THE GREAT PHILOSOPHERS

Consulting Editors
Ray Monk and Frederic Raphael

DATE DUE

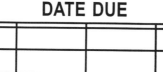

BERTRAND RUSSELL

Ray Monk

ROUTLEDGE
New York

Published in 1999 by
Routledge
29 West 35th Street
New York, NY 10001

First published in 1997 by
Phoenix
A Division of the Orion Publishing Group Ltd.
Orion House
5 Upper Saint Martin's Lane
London WC2H 9EA

10 9 8 7 6 5 4 3 2 1

Library of Congress Cataloging-in-Publication Data

Monk, Ray.
        Bertrand Russell / Ray Monk.
          p. cm.—(The great philosophers : 7)
        Includes bibliographical references.
        ISBN 0-415-92386-7 (pbk.)
        1. Mathematics—Philosophy. 2. Logic, Symbolic
        and mathematical. 3. Russell, Bertrand, 1872–1970.
        I. Title. II. Series: Great Philosophers (Routledge
        (Firm)) : 7.
QA8.4.M65 1999
510'.92—dc21   99-22642
                                                    CIP

ABBREVIATIONS OF RUSSELL'S WORKS USED IN THE TEXT

Auto 1   *The Autobiography of Bertrand Russell 1872–1914*, London, Allen and Unwin, 1967

Auto 3   *The Autobiography of Bertrand Russell Volume III, 1914–1944*, London, Allen and Unwin, 1968

CPBR 2   *The Collected Papers of Bertrand Russell 2*, London, Unwin Hyman, 1990

EA   *Essays in Analysis*, London, Allen and Unwin, 1973

HWP   *History of Western Philosophy*, London, Routledge, 1991

LA   *The Philosophy of Logical Atomism*, La Salle, Illinois, Open Court, 1985

ML   *Mysticism and Logic*, London, Unwin Paperbacks, 1976

MPD   *My Philosophical Development*, New York, Simon and Schuster, 1959

NEP   *Nightmares of Eminent Persons*, Harmondsworth, Penguin, 1962

POM   *The Principles of Mathematics*, London, Allen and Unwin, 1985

PM   *Principia Mathematica to *56*, Cambridge University Press, 1962

PFM   *Portraits from Memory*, London, Allen and Unwin, 1956

RUSSELL

Mathematics: Dreams and Nightmares

1
THE PYTHAGOREAN DREAM

'The first thing that led me to philosophy', Bertrand Russell wrote late in life, 'occurred at the age of eleven.' It was then that his older brother, Frank, taught him Euclid's system of geometry. As he describes it in his *Autobiography*

This was one of the great events of my life, as dazzling as first love. I had not imagined that there was anything so delicious in the world. After I had learned the fifth proposition, my brother told me that it was generally considered difficult, but I had found no difficulty whatever. This was the first time it had dawned upon me that I might have some intelligence. From that moment until Whitehead and I finished *Principia Mathematica*, when I was thirty-eight, mathematics was my chief interest, and my chief source of happiness. Like all happiness, however, it was not unalloyed. I had been told that Euclid proved things, and was much disappointed that he started with axioms. At first I refused to accept them unless my brother could offer me some reason for doing so, but he said: 'If you don't accept them we cannot go on', and as I wished to go on, I reluctantly accepted them *pro tem*. The doubt as to the premises of mathematics which I felt at that moment remained with me, and determined the course of my subsequent work.

(Auto I, 36)

'Dazzling' and 'delicious' are not words that one would normally associate with learning geometry, and yet Russell's rapturous reaction has an intriguing precedent. According to Aubrey's *Brief Lives*, when the seventeenth-century British philosopher Thomas Hobbes was forty years old, he happened to glance at a copy of Euclid's *Elements* that was lying open on a desk in a library he visited. It was open at the proof of the famous Pythagorean Theorem. 'By God, this is impossible!' Hobbes exclaimed:

> So he reads the Demonstration of it, which referred him back to such a Proposition; which proposition he read. That referred him back to another, which he also read. *Et sic deinceps* [and so on] that at last he was demonstratively convinced of that truth. This made him in love with Geometry.

For both Hobbes and Russell, the almost erotic delight they took in learning Euclid's geometry ('as dazzling as first love') was aroused by the feeling of finally coming to know something with complete certainty. The beauty of Euclid's system is that it is axiomatic. Everything that it teaches about circles, triangles, squares, etc. is not just stated but *proved*; complicated and surprising things about the relations between angles and lengths and so on are shown to be merely logical consequences of a few, simple axioms. It's as if a whole, vast body of knowledge has been spun out of virtually nothing, but, more than that, this body of

4

knowledge is not tenative or provisional, it does not depend upon the contingencies of the world, but rather can be established once and for all. If one accepts the axioms, one *has* to accept the rest; no further doubt is possible. To someone who wishes, as Russell passionately wished, to find *reasons* for their beliefs, the exhilarating possibility this opens up is that some beliefs at least can be provided with absolutely cast-iron foundations.

Bertrand Russell had special reason to find the experience of certain knowledge intoxicating, for, up until his introduction to Euclidean geometry, his world had been alarmingly changeable and shrouded in mystery. He was born in 1872 into one of the very grandest Whig families. His ancestor, John Russell, the first Earl of Bedford, was one of the richest and most powerful members of the new aristocracy created by Henry VIII, and his grandfather, Lord John Russell, had twice served as Prime Minister during Queen Victoria's reign. Russell was brought up fully conscious of the proud tradition into which he had been born – he once said that he was raised to live his life in such a way that after his death an equestrian statue would be built in his honour – but he was also brought up in almost complete ignorance of his parents. His mother and his sister died when he was two, and his father a year later, leaving him in the care of his grandparents. When he was six, his grandfather died, leaving him in the sole care of his grandmother, Countess Russell. After this, he later said, he ~~u~~sed to lie awake at night wondering when she too would ~~die~~ and leave him.

This series of bereavements was dreadful enough, but what made the situation much worse was that his grandmother learned that Russell's mother had had an affair with Douglas Spalding, a tutor the Russells had hired to teach their children. Lady Russell's shock at this was such that she hardly mentioned Russell's parents to him and when she did, it was to hint that he had had a lucky escape not to have been brought up by such wicked people. As a result, Russell 'vaguely sensed a dark mystery' about his parents and, as a child, spent much time alone in his garden wondering what sort of people they had been and why his grandmother maintained a disapproving silence about them.

Against the background of such awful loss, uncertainty and the frustrated yearning to know something about his parents, the experience of discovering a realm of truth free from the vicissitudes of human existence was ecstatic to Russell, and it inspired in him a desire to found *all* knowledge upon the kind of rock-solid foundations provided by Euclid's system of geometry.

I found great delight in mathematics – much more delight, in fact, than in any other study. I liked to think of the applications of mathematics to the physical world, and I hoped that in time there would be a mathematics of human behaviour as precise as the mathematics of machines. I hoped this because I liked demonstrations, and at most times this motive outweighed the desire, which I also felt, to believe in free will.

(*PFM*, 20)

But, apart from the hope it aroused of applying mathematics to the physical world and to human behaviour, there was another aspect to the delight that the young Russell found in Euclidean geometry that was to influence his philosophical development enormously, and that was the introduction it provided him to what philosophers often call 'Plato's World of Ideas'. As he was later to put it in *History of Western Philosophy*:

> Mathematics is, I believe, the chief source of the belief in eternal and exact truth, as well as in a super-sensible intelligible world. Geometry deals with exact circles, but no sensible object is *exactly* circular; however carefully we may use our compasses, there will be some imperfections and irregularities. This suggests the view that all exact reasoning applies to ideal as opposed to sensible objects; it is natural to go further, and to argue that thought is nobler than sense, and the objects of thought more real than those of sense-perception.
>
> (*HWP*, 55–6)

In his essay, 'Why I took to Philosophy', Russell made clear the importance this form of mysticism had for his own philosophical motivations:

> For a time I found satisfaction in a doctrine derived, with modification, from Plato. According to Plato's doctrine, which I accepted only in a watered-down form, there is an unchanging timeless world of ideas of which the world presented to our senses is an imperfect copy. Mathematics, according to this doctrine, deals with the

world of ideas and has in consequence an exactness and perfection which is absent from the everyday world. This kind of mathematical mysticism, which Plato derived from Pythagoras, appealed to me.

(PFM, 22)

In *My Philosophical Development*, he was blunter: 'I disliked the real world and sought refuge in a timeless world, without change or decay or the will-o'-the-wisp of progress' (*MPD*, 210).

Though the notion of a world of ideas, in which truths are timeless and discoverable by reason alone, is more commonly associated with Plato, Russell always insisted on attributing it to Pythagoras, who thus became for him a figure of emblematic importance, 'intellectually one of the most important men that ever lived', as Russell describes him in *History of Western Philosophy*. Pythagoras is an elusive figure in the history of philosophy; no text of his has survived and little is known of his life. It is generally agreed that he lived from about 550 to 500 BC, but that is almost where the agreement stops, and most of what Russell says about Pythagoras's philosophy has been disputed by other scholars. Nevertheless, what Russell believed about Pythagoras was of great importance to him, because it fixed Pythagoras as the type of philosopher Russell aspired to be and gave shape to the dream which Russell pursued in his philosophy of mathematics.

As Russell presents him, Pythagoras was both a religious prophet and a pure mathematician: 'In both respects h was immeasurably influential, and the two were not separate as they seem to a modern mind.' Pythagoras's religion, according to Russell, was a reformed version of Orphism, which was, in turn, a reformed version of the worship of Dionysus. Central to all three was the exaltation of ecstasy, but in the cult of Pythagoras, this ecstasy is to be achieved not by drinking wine or indulging in sexual activity, but rather by the exercise of the intellect. The highest life, on this view, is that devoted to 'passionate sympathetic contemplation', which Russell (following F.M. Cornford) says was the original meaning of the word 'theory'.

> For Pythagoras, the 'passionate contemplation' was intellectual, and issued in mathematical knowledge. In this way, through Pythagoreanism, 'theory' gradually acquired its modern meaning; but for all who were inspired by Pythagoras it retained an element of ecstatic revelation. To those who have reluctantly learnt a little mathematics in school this may seem strange; but to those who have experienced the intoxicating delight of sudden understanding that mathematics gives, from time to time, to those who love it, the Pythagoras view will seem completely natural, even if untrue. It might seem that the empirical philosopher is the slave of his material, but the pure mathematician, like the musician, is a free creator of his world of ordered beauty.
>
> (*HWP*, 52–3)

Pythagoras ('as everyone knows', according to Russell) believed that 'all things are numbers'. Everything in the world, whether it be the building of pyramids, the things of nature, the harmonies of music, or whatever, expresses a series of numerical relations, and can be described by those relations. The tragedy for the Pythagoreans (and, as we shall see, a similar tragedy was played out in Russell's own philosophical development) was that their greatest, most well-known discovery was the one that undermined this point of view: namely the famous Pythagorean Theorem concerning right-angled triangles, which led immediately to the discovery of incommensurables.

According to the Pythagorean Theorem, the length of the hypotenuse of a right-angled triangle in which the other two sides are one unit long will be equal to the square root of 2. The trouble is that the square root of 2 is incommensurable; that is, it cannot be expressed as the relation between two numbers, or, to put it another way, it is 'irrational'. It follows that there is at least one thing in the world which is *not* the expression of a numerical relation. Others, of course, followed; the best known of which is *pi*, the relation between the circumference and the diameter of a circle. To the ancient Greeks, this suggested that geometry, not arithmetic, was the surest source of exact knowledge, which is one reason for the pre-eminence given to Euclid's *Elements*.

The Pythagorean Dream of showing everything to be reducible to arithmetic was, it seemed, over. New mathematical techniques, however, developed during the Scientific Revolution of the seventeenth and eighteenth centuries, served to revive the dream, at least to the extent of re-establishing arithmetic as the supreme form of mathematics. Chief among these were the co-ordinate geometry introduced by Descartes, which allowed geometrical theorems to be expressed and proved arithmetically, and the differential calculus, developed (independently) by Newton and Leibniz, which enabled mathematics, for the first time, to represent *motion* arithmetically, thus providing the sciences of mechanics, dynamics and physics with an immensely powerful new tool. The problem of incommensurables, however, continued to haunt those who looked to mathematics for perfect rigour and exactitude. Quantities like $\sqrt{2}$ and *pi* were included in the domain of 'real' numbers, though no satisfactory definition of them – or, therefore, of the notion of a 'real number' in general – was yet available. And, indeed, the new techniques brought with them further problems in trying to make sense of the world of numbers, problems which opened up the science of mathematics to the charge of being riddled with inconsistencies.

Three fundamental notions in mathematics – infinity, the infinitesimal, and continuity – seemed inherently paradoxical. The paradoxes of infinity and continuity had been known since ancient times, but they acquired a new importance as the power of mathematics to represent continuous and infinite sequences grew. Both take many forms. The form of the paradox of infinity that especially worried Leibniz was this: even numbers are only a part, a half, of the whole realm of whole numbers (which, of course, includes both odd and even numbers), and yet, to every whole number we can assign a corresponding even number:

1	2	3	4	5	6	.	.	.
2	4	6	8	10	12	.	.	.

The two sets, in other words, can be put into a *one-to-one correspondence*. But, surely, two sets can only be paired off in this way if they have the *same* number of members (in a monogamous society, for example, we know that the number of wives is equal to the number of husbands, since to each member of one set there corresponds a member of the other). How can the set of even numbers be, at one and the same time, both *smaller than* and *the same size as* the set of natural numbers? The problem arises, of course, from the fact that both sets are infinite (even though one is a proper sub-set of the other), which led many philosophers to conclude that the notion of infinity is inherently contradictory.

The paradoxes of continuity had been known since antiquity and were associated with a disciple of Paramenides called Zeno, who had used them to argue that there was no such thing as motion. They arise from considering a continuous line as a sequence of discrete points. The problem is that this sequence must be infinitely divisible. Take, for example, the flight of an arrow. Before it reaches its target, Zeno argued, it must reach a point halfway towards its target; but, before it can reach *that* point, it must reach a point halfway to it, and so on *ad infinitum*. As the chain of presuppositions involved in the claim that the arrow moves never comes to an end, its supposed motion can never begin and thus, Zeno urges, must be regarded as illusory. Despite what we appear to see with our own eyes, reason will tell us that the arrow never moves! Few have been prepared to accept this conclusion, but the mathematical difficulty it raises of how a continuous quantity can be understood as a sequence of discrete points remained unsolved until the nineteenth century.

Related to the problems of continuity were those surrounding the notion of an infinitesimal, a notion that plays a central role in the differential calculus, as originally devised. An infinitesimal is supposed to be an infinitely small quantity, smaller than any quantity one could think of and yet not nothing. It cannot be nothing, since continuous lines are regarded as being made up of them. And yet, in the calculation of a derivative – in, for example, the calculation of the velocity of a moving object at a certain point in time – an infinitesimal quantity is treated as no quantity at all. This process, though it works in practice, is quite manifestly inconsistent, and was famously ridiculed by Bishop Berkeley in his attack on Newton's calculus, *The Analyst*. What are these 'evanescent Increments' used in the calculus? Berkeley sneered. 'They are neither finite Quantities, nor Quantities infinitely small nor yet not nothing. May we not call them the Ghosts of departed Quantities?' Anyone who could accept such a notion, Berkeley suggested, ought to have no qualms in accepting the mysteries of Christianity, for do not mathematicians have their own mysteries, 'and what is more, their repugnancies and contradictions?'

By the middle of the nineteenth century, these embarrassing logical problems at the heart of mathematics had inspired a movement, led by German mathematicians, to inspired a movement, led by German mathematicians, to provide mathematics, and particularly the calculus, with more rigorous foundations. Despite his passion for mathematics, however, Russell did not learn of the work of these mathematicians until after he had finished his mathematics studies at Cambridge. When he did learn of it, it changed his philosophical outlook fundmentally. Much to Russell's disgust, the mathematics that he was taught, both prior to and during his time as an undergraduate, treated the subject, not in the Pythagorean spirit as the establishment of exact truths concerning the abstract world of ideas, but rather in a more pragmatic spirit as a series of useful techniques.

Those who taught me the infinitesimal Calculus did not know the valid proofs of its fundamental theorems and tried to persuade me to accept the official sophistries as an act of faith. I realized that the calculus works in practice, but I was at a loss to understand why it should do so. However, I found so much pleasure in the acquisition of technical skill that at most times I forgot my doubts. (*MPD*, 35–6)

... The mathematical teaching at Cambridge when I was an undergraduate was definitely bad. Its badness was partly due to the order of merit in the Tripos, which was abolished not long afterwards. The necessity for nice discrimination between the abilities of different examinees led to an emphasis on 'problems' as opposed to 'bookwork'. The 'proofs' that were offered of mathematical theorems were an insult to the logical intelligence.

Indeed, the whole subject of mathematics was taught as a set of clever tricks by which to pile up marks in the Tripos. The effect of all this upon me was to make me think mathematics disgusting. When I had finished my Tripos, I sold all my mathematical books and made a vow that I would never look at a mathematical book again. And so, in my fourth year, I plunged with whole-hearted delight into the fantastic world of philosophy.

(*MPD*, 37–8)

Despairing of mathematics as it was then taught, Russell looked to metaphysics to satisfy the Pythagorean yearnings that his intoxication with Euclidean geometry had aroused in him. He began philosophy in 1893 and within a year had chosen to concentrate on the subject that had first inspired his hopes of finding exact and certain knowledge: the foundations of geometry. Now, however, he sought those foundations not in mathematics, but in philosophy, and in particular in a form of Kantian transcendental idealism. In *Critique of Pure Reason*, Kant had raised the following problem: how can the theorems of Euclidean geometry be established on the basis of reason alone and yet hold true for the physical world? Most of the things we know about the physical world have to be arrived at by observation and experiment; how is it that such truths as, for example, the Pythagorean Theorem can be known *a priori*, without reference to our experience of the world? Kant concluded that Euclidean geometry describes not the world as it is in itself, but the world as it appears to us. The world does not *have* to be as Euclid describes it, but we *have* to see and imagine it as such. We look at the world, so to speak, through Euclidean spectacles. Or, to put it into Kantian jargon, what Euclidean geometry describes is our 'form of intuition' with regard to space. That is why the theorems of Euclidean geometry look to us as if they were *necessarily* true, as if, like the principles of logic, their truth was guaranteed by the nature of reason itself.

Some doubt was thrown on this view after Kant's death by the creation of alternative systems of geometry, so-called *non-Euclidean* geometries. Of these, the two most famous were those created by the German mathematician, Georg Riemann, and the Russian, Nikolai Lobachevsky. Both these systems dropped Euclid's fifth postulate (the one that ensures that parallel lines never meet) and produced in consequence descriptions of 'curved' space. In this kind of space, everything is different; the angles of a triangle, for example, do not add up to 180 degrees, but either slightly more (in the case of Riemannian geometry) or slightly less (in Lobachevskyan). Given that these systems are internally consistent (which they are) and that we can imagine the spaces they describe (which is often disputed), it looks as though Kant was wrong: we do not *have* to perceive the world as Euclidean. Why should we not see it as Riemannian or Lobachevskyan? This also threatens the thought that had excited the eleven-year-old Bertrand Russell, the thought that we can know, *a priori* and with complete certainty and exactitude, the spatial relations that exist in the physical world.

In his first philosophical book, *The Foundations of Geometry*, Russell responded to this dilemma in a quasi-Kantian manner. What Kant had claimed for Euclidean geometry, Russell argued, is in fact true of the relatively recent subject of projective geometry, which studies geometrical figures not in regard to their size but only with respect to their shape, their 'congruence' with each other. The axioms of projective geometry would be true whether space was curved or not, so long as its curvature was constant. Whether Euclid, Riemann or Lobachevsky has given us a correct description of physical space is, Russell thus claimed, an empirical matter, but what we *can* know with certainty is that *if* space is curved, its curvature is constant. To understand the issue involved here, think of the difference between the surface of a football and the surface of an egg. If you drew a triangle on a football, you could imagine sliding that triangle around the surface of the ball without having to distort its shape; a triangle in one part of the football would, that is, be *congruent* with a triangle in another. But now imagine drawing a triangle on the fat end of an egg and trying to slide it towards the thin end: the triangle would have to change its shape. This is because the space on the surface of an egg, though curved, does not curve constantly. Whatever real physical space is like, Russell maintained, it *cannot* be like the surface of an egg. Unfortunately for this view, the space of relativity theory *is* like the surface of an egg, its curvature varying with respect to varying degrees of mass gravitational force. Russell's earliest published philosophical theory, therefore, is now regarded as one of the few philosophical theories capable of conclusive scientific refutation.

In later life, Russell was dismissive of his earlier work on time of its publication he considered himself to be on the brink of realising through philosophical Idealism something like the Pythagorean Dream of revealing a rational reality of eternal truths behind the messy appearance of contingent facts. This reality, however, was to be apprehended not through geometry or through arithmetic, but rather through logic and, in particular, through the dialectical kind of logic introduced into philosophy by the German Absolute Idealist, Friedrich Hegel. This kind of logic arrives at conclusions not by ordinary inference, but by a process of *synthesis* that seeks to overcome contradictions by bringing opposites together to form new 'transcendent' unities. Eventually, in Hegel's philosophy, this process reaches the conclusion that Reality as a whole is one Absolute Idea.

Russell's conversion to neo-Hegelianism came about through his contact with J.M.E. McTaggart, whose *Studies in the Hegelian Dialectic* was widely influential among Cambridge philosophers of the 1890s. McTaggart's emphasis was on the interconnectedness of everything in the world as perceived by Hegel's philosophy. Separateness, according to this doctrine, is an illusion, and is shown to be such by a dialectic that proceeds from the lower categories of understanding – things like space, time and matter – to the highest, the Absolute. Only this latter is independent and real, and only this is rational; all the lower categories are enmeshed in contradictions that are resolved by successive synthesis until one reaches the Absolute. In this vision (analogous, in this respect, to the Pythagorean Dream), logic and religion meet, for the logic of this dialectic shows us that, in McTaggart's words, 'all reality is rational and righteous ... the highest object of philosophy is to indicate to us the general nature of an ultimate harmony, the full content of which it has not yet entered into our hearts to conceive'. 'All true philosophy', McTaggart declares, 'must be mystical, not indeed in its methods, but in its final conclusions.'

For a short period, Russell was inspired by this peculiar form of mysticism to embrace an ambitious scheme of writing a 'dialectic of the sciences' that would, by successively exposing the contradiction inherent in mathematics, physics and the other sciences, demonstrate the superiority of Hegelian philosophy over all over attempts to make sense of the world. His work during this period (most of which remained unpublished) contains repeated admonitions to mathematicians for refusing to acknowledge the logical contradictions that beset their subject. For example, in a paper he wrote in 1896 called 'On Some Difficulties of Continuous Quantity', he begins:

From Zeno onwards, the difficulties of continua have been felt by philosophers, and evaded, with ever subtler analysis, by mathematicians ... it seemed worth while to collect and define, as briefly as possible, some contradictions in the relation of continuous quantity to number, and also to show, what mathematicians are in danger of forgetting, that philosophical antinomies, in this sphere, find their counterpart in mathematical fallacies. These fallacies seem, to me at least, to pervade the Calculus.

(*CPBR 2*, 46)

In other words, bad philosophy – or worse, indifference to philosophy – produces bad mathematics (the 'official sophistries' and 'clever tricks' of which he had complained earlier). If mathematicians genuinely wanted to understand mathematical truth, they would do well to turn their attention to the contradictions of continuity, infinity and the infinitesimal and rethink the logical and philosophical foundations of their subject.

As Russell belatedly began to discover in the last few years of the nineteenth century, mathematicians, particularly German mathematicians, had been doing just that for some time. As a result of the work of Weierstrass, Dedekind and Cantor, pure mathematics had been provided with much more sophisticated foundations. The notion of an infinitesimal had been banished, 'real' numbers had been provided with a logically consistent definition, continuity had been redefined and, more controversially, a whole new branch of arithmetic had been invented ('transfinite arithmetic') which addressed itself to the paradoxes of infinity. Many philosophers have regarded the picture of the mathematical realm that results from all this work as even more bewildering than that that emerges from the mathematics of Newton and Leibniz. Wittgenstein, for example, has described the entire body of work of these German mathematicians as a 'cancerous growth'. And, it is true, it offends common sense at almost every point. It requires, for example, one to believe that there exist *different* infinities so that, for example, the number of points in a continuum is greater than the number of natural numbers, though both are infinite. It also requires one to embrace precisely the conclusions that had previously been thought paradoxical: for example, that in a continuous series of points there is no such thing as 'the next' point, so that, as Russell once put it, Zeno's arrow 'at every moment of its flight, is truly at rest'.

For Russell, however, the abandonment of common sense was a small price to pay for a logically consistent theory of mathematics. He never much cared for common sense anyway, declaring it to be the 'metaphysics of savages'. His joy at discovering *mathematical* solutions to the logical problems of mathematics was almost unconfined and within a couple years of first being acquainted with the work of Weierstrass, Cantor and Dedekind, he abandoned altogether the neo-Hegelianism of his 'dialectic of the sciences'. 'Mathematics', he now believed, 'could be *quite* true, and not merely a stage in dialectic', and he had no further use for 'the Absolute'. This produced a fundamental change in his philosophical outlook, what he would later call the 'one major division' in his thinking. There were, Russell was fond of saying, just two types of philosopher: those who think of the world as a bowl of jelly and those who think of it as a bucket of shot. Having, through the work of modern mathematicians, rediscovered his faith in *analysis*, Russell could give up the jelly and embrace the shot. The task of philosophy, then, was no longer to demonstrate the interconnectedness of everything, to prove that Reality was an indivisible whole; rather the task was to identify, through analysis, the discrete atoms –

material, psychological and logical – of which the world is constructed.

With regard to mathematics, this enabled Russell to adopt a very robust form of Pythagoreanism: there really is a mathematical realm, and its truths are indeed discoverable through reason alone. All the old barriers to believing this – problems of incommensurables, the paradoxes of continuity, infinity and the infinitesimal – had been overcome, and there was no longer any need to resort to Idealism, whether Kantian or Hegelian, to make sense of mathematics: ordinary (not dialectical) logic was enough. Russell's delight in this aroused in him an unrestrained triumphalism:

> One of the chief triumphs of modern mathematics consists in having discovered what mathematics really is ... All pure mathematics – Arithmetic, Analysis, and Geometry – is built up by combinations of the primitive ideas of logic, and its propositions are deduced from the general axioms of logic, such as the syllogism and the other rules of inference. And this is no longer a dream or an aspiration. On the contrary, over the greater and more difficult part of the domain of mathematics, it has already been accomplished; in the remaining cases, there is no special difficulty, and it is now being rapidly achieved. Philosophers have disputed for ages whether such deduction was possible; mathematicians have sat down and made the deduction. For the philosophers there is now nothing left but graceful acknowledgements.

... Zeno was concerned ... with three problems, each presented by motion, but each more abstract than motion, and capable of a purely arithmetical treatment. There are the problems of the infinitesimal, the infinite, and continuity. To state clearly the difficulties involved was to accomplish perhaps the hardest part of the philosopher's task. This was done by Zeno. From him to our own day, the finest intellects of each generation in turn attacked the problems, but achieved, broadly speaking, nothing. In our own time, however, three men – Weierstrass, Dedekind, and Cantor – have not merely advanced the three problems, but have completely solved them. The solutions, for those acquainted with mathematics, are so clear as to leave no longer the slightest doubt or difficulty. This achievement is probably the greatest of which our age has to boast; and I know of no age (except perhaps the golden age of Greece) which has a more convincing proof to offer of the transcendent genius of its great men.

(ML, 76–82)

Russell's conversion from synthesis to analysis, and from Idealism to Realism, is more frequently credited to the influence of G.E. Moore, but the impact of the work of Weierstrass, Cantor and Dedekind was, in fact, far greater. In the final chapter of his *History of Western Philosophy*, Russell extols the achievements of analytic philosophy (or 'the philosophy of logical analysis', as he calls it) and though he does not mention Moore at all, he emphasizes the importance of the work of these German mathematicians. 'The origin of this philosophy', he writes, 'is in the achievements of mathematicians who set to work to purge their subject of fallacies and slipshod reasoning.'

Russell's greatest work in philosophy was inspired by the example of these mathematicians. They had shown that mathematics was logically consistent – or, in any case, they had removed what were, historically, the most important reasons for thinking that it was not – what Russell now dreamed of was a demonstration that mathematics *was* logic. The vision that opened up to him was of an axiomatic system, more rigorous even than Euclid's, in which the *whole* of mathematics could be spun out of a few trivial axioms. These axioms would not be specifically mathematical, they would not mention points, straight lines, or even numbers; they would be simple truths of logic, things like: if p implies q, and q implies r, then p implies r. In this way, mathematics would be shown not only to be free from contradiction, but also to be absolutely and irrefragably *true*. A vast realm of knowledge would have been shown to be immune to any sceptical doubt whatsoever.

Russell's immediate starting point in this quest was the mathematical logic of the Italian mathematician Giuseppe Peano, whom Russell met at an academic congress in Paris in 1900. 'I was impressed', Russell later said, 'by the fact that, in every discussion, he [Peano] showed more precision and more logical rigour than was shown by anybody else. I went to him and said, "I wish to read all your works. Have you got copies with you?" He had, and I immediately read them all.' By using a specially invented logical notation (the basic elements of which are still in use today and familiar to all undergraduate students of formal logic), Peano was able to show that the whole of arithmetic could be founded upon a system that used only three basic notions and five initial axioms. His three basic notions were: zero, number, and 'successor of', and his five axioms were:

1. 0 is a number
2. If x is a number, the successor of x is a number
3. If two numbers have the same successor, the two numbers are identical
4. 0 is not the successor of any number
5. If S is a class containing 0 and the successor of every number belonging to S, then S contains all numbers

To reduce the whole of arithmetic to such a small handful of initial assumptions was a tremendous achievement and Russell was fulsome in his praise of it. Peano, he wrote, is 'the great master of the art of formal reasoning, among the men of our own day'. But, Russell thought, Peano had not *quite* reached logical rock-bottom; Peano's basic notions, he was convinced, could be reduced yet further by defining them in terms of the logically still more primitive notion of *class*. If an axiomatic theory of classes could be constructed in which Peano's basic notions were definable and his five axioms demonstrable, then, Russell reasoned, arithmetic could be shown to be nothing more than a branch of logic. This is the central idea of Russell's great work, *The Principles of Mathematics*, the first draft of which he finished at the end of 1900, just months after his meeting with Peano, but which was not finally published until 1903, by which time Russell's Pythagorean visions had received a mortal blow.

Unlike the mathematician who inspired him, Russell was motivated by primarily philosophical considerations. For him, a large part of the purpose of deriving mathematics from logic was to show that the Kantian philosophy of mathematics – and still more, of course, the Hegelian philosophy – was false. If mathematics is a branch of logic, Russell believed, then Kant's appeal to subjective, psychological notions like 'forms of intuition' was unnecessary. *The Principles of Mathematics* thus begins with a trenchant and self-confident dismissal of Kant's philosophy of mathematics, and a bold statement of both the definitive correctness and the philosophical importance of the thesis that mathematics is logic:

> The Philosophy of Mathematics has been hitherto as controversial and unprogressive as the other branches of philosophy. Although it was generally agreed that mathematics is in some sense true, philosophers disputed as to what mathematical propositions really meant; although something was true, no two people were agreed as to what it was that was true, and if something was known, no two people were agreed as to what it was that was known. So long, however, as this was doubtful, it could hardly be said that any certain and exact knowledge was to be had in mathematics. We find, accordingly, that idealists have tended more and

more to regard all mathematics as dealing with mere appearance, while empiricists have held everything mathematical to be approximation to some exact truth about which they had nothing to tell us. This state of things, it must be confessed, was thoroughly unsatisfactory. Philosophy asks of Mathematics: What does it mean? Mathematics in the past was unable to answer, and Philosophy answered by introducing the totally irrelevant notion of mind. But now Mathematics is able to answer, so far at least as to reduce the whole of its propositions to certain fundamental notions of logic. At this point, the discussion must be resumed by Philosophy. I shall endeavour to indicate what are the fundamental notions involved, to prove at length that no others occur in mathematics, and to point out briefly the philosophical difficulties involved in the analysis of these notions. A complete treatment of these difficulties would involve a treatise on Logic, which will not be found in the following pages.

There was, until very lately, a special difficulty in the principles of mathematics. It seemed plain that mathematics consisted of deductions, and yet the orthodox accounts of deduction were largely or wholly inapplicable to existing mathematics. Not only the Aristotelian syllogistic theory, but also the modern doctrines of Symbolic Logic, were either theoretically inadequate to mathematical reasoning, or at any rate required such artificial forms of statement that they could not be practically applied. In this fact lay the strength of the

Kantian view, which asserted that mathematical reasoning is not strictly formal, but always uses intuitions, *i.e.*, the *a priori* knowledge of space and time. Thanks to the progress of Symbolic Logic, especially as treated by Professor Peano, this part of the Kantian philosophy is now capable of a final and irrevocable refutation. By the help of ten principles of deduction and ten other premises of a general logical nature (*e.g.*, 'implication is a relation'), all mathematics can be strictly and formally deduced; and all the entities that occur in the mathematics can be defined in terms of those that occur in the above twenty premises. In this statement, Mathematics includes not only Arithmetic and Analysis, but also Geometry, Euclidean and non-Euclidean, rational Dynamics, and an indefinite number of other studies still unborn or in their infancy. The fact that all Mathematics is Symbolic Logic is one of the greatest discoveries of our age; and when this fact has been established, the remainder of the principles of mathematics consists in the analysis of Symbolic Logic itself.

(*POM*, 4–5)

The Principles of Mathematics is a difficult book, full of abstruse and sophisticated reasoning, and written in a more technical and formal style than had been, up until then, customary in philosophical literature. However, it is not a work either of formal logic or of mathematics, and Russell does not actually construct the system of logic to which he claims mathematics to be reducible, nor does he attempt to carry out the reduction. His aim is rather to argue that such a reduction is possible. He does, however, specify the basic notions and the axioms that his preferred system of logic would contain. Of central importance to Russell is the notion of a *class*, which, it is important to realize, is rather different from the notion of a set, as that appears in mathematics. Set Theory had been a branch of mathematics for some time before *The Principles of Mathematics* was written and if all Russell was proposing was that mathematics be reduced to Set Theory, that would not have had the momentous philosophical importance that Russell claimed for his work; it would simply be to reduce the whole of mathematics to one particular branch of it. What Russell was proposing was a demonstration that mathematics could be reduced to *logic*, and it was thus vital to him that he should begin with a purely *logical* notion.

What, then, is the difference between a set and a class? A set, typically, is defined by enumeration: {2,4,6}, for example, is a set containing three members. Russell, originally, had difficulty in accepting Cantor's transfinite set theory, because he could not see how an infinite *set* could be well defined, for clearly we cannot enumerate the members of an infinite collection. One of the things he got from Peano, however, which helped him overcome these doubts, was the rather different notion of *class*, which is defined, not in terms of its members, but rather in terms of what is called a *propositional function*. Broadly speaking, a propositional function is a proposition with a variable. 'Plato is a man' and 'Socrates is a man' are propositions, but 'x is a man' is a propositional function. The class of men is then defined as the things of which 'x is a man' is true, *whatever they may be*. To grasp the notion of 'the class of men', we do not need to know how many members the class has, nor whether the number of members is infinite, nor even if it has any members at all; we only need to know what the propositional function 'x is a man' *means*. Thus 'class' is a purely logical notion, derived not only from a branch of mathematics, but from quite general considerations about propositions: every meaningful proposition has a form that can be expressed by a propositional function, and to every propositional function there corresponds a class.

Essentially, Russell's task in reducing Peano's system of arithmetic to a system of logic was to show how Peano's three basic notions and five basic axioms could be recast in terms of classes. In other words, he had to demonstrate that numbers could be defined as classes. He did this by taking as fundamental the notion of a *one-to-one correspondence* between classes, and adopting Cantor's idea that two classes were *equinumerous* (or 'similar' as Russell puts it) if they could be put into such a correspondence. A number is then defined as a class of 'similar' classes: the number 3, for example, would be the class of classes having three members. 0 is the class of empty classes, and 1 is the class of classes containing only a single member. Having defined 0 and 1, Russell is able to define the notion '+1' (Peano's notion of 'successor') and thus all five of Peano's axioms.

From this basis, Russell goes on to define rational numbers, irrational numbers, real numbers, complex numbers, transfinite numbers and continuity. He also gives a sketch of how ordinary geometry, projective geometry, the differential calculus, Newton's Laws of Motion and Heinrich Hertz's Theory of Dynamics would appear within his theory. The scope of the book, and of his ambition, was breathtakingly large. As he put it in a letter to a friend: 'I invented a new subject, which turned out to be all mathematics, for the first time treated in its essence.' He had, he believed, shown what mathematics really was and in doing so, he had realized his and Pythagoras's dream of revealing it to be a body of abstract yet objective truth, our knowledge of which was perfectly and apodictically demonstrable. Intellectually, he later said, the writing of the first draft of *The Principles of Mathematics* was 'the highest point of my life', an 'intellectual honeymoon such as I have never experienced before or since':

Every day I found myself understanding something that I had not understood on the previous day. I thought all difficulties were solved and all problems were at an end.

(*MPD*, 73)

But, he adds, 'the honeymoon could not last, and early in the following year intellectual sorrow descended upon me in full measure.'

2
THE MATHEMATICIAN'S NIGHTMARE

Russell's 'intellectual honeymoon' came to an end with his nightmarish discovery that the notion of a class, to which he had wanted to reduce the whole of mathematics, was itself contradictory. To understand the impact this discovery had on him, one has to retrace his thoughts concerning classes. According to Russell's version of Pythagoras's mathematical mysticism, classes were a kind of object. They were not, to be sure, the kind of object that can be seen or touched, but nevertheless they had for him a real, objective existence. They did not exist 'in the mind', but in, so to speak, the 'world of forms'. They had, that is, the kind of existence that Pythagoras and Plato had claimed for numbers; indeed, *exactly* the same kind of existence, since for Russell, numbers *were* classes. Numbers, on Russell's theory, were classes *of classes*, and this, for Russell, meant that classes had to be some kind of object, for otherwise how could one form classes *of* them?

That there was something wrong with this conception of class was suggested to Russell by his reflections upon Cantor's theory of infinite sets. Cantor had a famous proof that there is no such thing as the highest cardinal number. A *cardinal* number is a number that is used to answer the question: how many? For example, if you count the number of people in a room and come to, say, 4, then the number 4 is being used as a cardinal. If, on the other hand, you were to put the people in a queue, and say: 'You're first, you're second, you're third, and you're fourth', then you would be using 1, 2, 3 and 4 as *ordinal* numbers. In Cantor's theory, cardinal numbers belong to sets, and there are infinite as well as finite cardinals. The set of natural numbers, for example, has an infinite cardinal – to which Cantor assigned the symbol $\aleph_0$ – and so does the set of real numbers. But Cantor had a proof – eventually accepted by Russell – that the set of real numbers has *more* members than the set of natural numbers. This proof works by demonstrating first that the natural numbers are a proper sub-set of the reals, and second that the reals *cannot* be put into a one-to-one correspondence with the naturals. It follows, Cantor argues, that the set of reals is *bigger than* the set of naturals.

Cantor also had a proof that, in general, a set has fewer members than its *power set* (that is, its set of subjects). If a set has n members, then there will be 2^n subsets of it, and 2^n is always greater than n. Putting these two together, Cantor concluded that the set of real numbers has the cardinal number $2^{\aleph_0}$. From here, Cantor constructed an entire hierarchy of different infinite numbers that can be continued indefinitely. There cannot be a greatest infinite cardinal number, Cantor reasoned, because *whatever* cardinal number one may take, one can always construct a larger one by forming its power set.

In the first flush of his enthusiasm for the work of Weierstrass, Dedekind and Cantor, Russell was convinced that there must be some mistake in this reasoning. Surely, he argued, if numbers are classes and classes are 'things', there *must* be a greater number, the number, that is, of total number of 'things' that exist (not in the physical world – for presumably that number is finite – but in the world of forms in which classes have their existence). As he put it in 1900:

> There is a greatest of all infinite numbers, which is the number of things altogether, of every sort and kind. It is obvious that there cannot be a greater number than this, because, if everything has been taken, there is nothing left to add. Cantor has a proof that there is no greatest number, and if this proof were valid, the contradictions of infinity would reappear in a sublimated form. But in this one point, the master has been guilty of a very subtle fallacy, which I hope to explain in some future work. (*ML*, 88)

Russell could, not, at first, accept Cantor's proof, because to do so would be to admit that the theory of classes contains a contradiction. The contradiction arises from considering the class of *all* classes. Surely this class has the highest cardinal number there could be, since numbers are classes and this class contains every class – and therefore every number – there could possibly be. But if Cantor is right, there is a simple method of constructing a larger class; namely by collecting together all of its sub-sets. But, if this *is* a larger class, then it could not be contained in the 'class of all classes', and how could the class of all classes *not* contain all classes?

After Russell had tried and failed to find a flaw in Cantor's argument, he reluctantly accepted its paradoxical consequence, and indeed, in his *Lectures on Logical Atomism*, made it the basis for what is surely one of the cleverest (though, admittedly, not one of the funniest) jokes in the literature of philosophy:

Every class of things that you can choose to mention has some cardinal number. That follows very easily from the definition of cardinal numbers as classes of similar classes, and you would be inclined to suppose that the class of all the things there are in the world would have about as many members as a class could be reasonably expected to have. The plain man would suppose you could not get a larger class than the class of all the things there are in the world. On the other hand, it is very easy to prove that if you take selections of some of the members of a class, making those selections in every conceivable way that you can, the number of different selections that you can make is greater than the original number of terms ... Generally speaking, if you have n terms, you can make 2^n selections. It is very easy to prove that 2^n is always greater than n, whether n happens to be finite or not. So you find that the total number of things in the world is not so great as the number of classes that can be made up out of those things. I am asking you to take all these propositions for granted, because there is not time to go into the proofs, but they are all in Cantor's work. Therefore you will find that the total number of things in the world is by no means the greatest number. On the contrary, there is a hierarchy of numbers greater than that. That, on the face of it, seems to land you in a contradiction. You have, in fact, a perfectly precise arithmetical proof that there are *fewer* things in heaven or earth than are dreamt of in *our* philosophy. That shows you how philosophy advances.

(*LA*, 129–30)

Actually, Russell's own philosophy advanced by ridding itself of this luxuriant ontology. If Cantor's proof is valid, he reasoned, then classes could not be objects; they were not, after all, among the 'things in the world'. Classes were, he now declared, 'logical fictions', and so were numbers: the Pythagorean world was, at least in part, an illusion.

He was strengthened in this view by his discovery of a contradiction in the notion of class that seemed more fundamental even than the paradox of the largest cardinal. This contradiction is now known as 'Russell's Paradox', and has become Russell's best known contribution to mathematical logic. It arises from the following considerations. The 'class of all classes' that Russell had been led to think about in his reflections on Cantor would be unusual among classes in having *itself* as a member. Most classes, clearly, are *not* members of themselves: the class of men, for example, is not a man. Now, suppose we construct the 'class of all classes that do not contain themselves' (that is, so to speak, the class of all *normal* classes), and ask: is that class a member of itself or not? We arrive at a logical impasse: if it is a member of itself, then it is not, and if it is not, then it is.

If Russell's delight in contemplating the world of mathematics could be regarded – as he himself was inclined to regard it – as a kind of religon, then these paradoxes brought him to the brink of atheism. He felt about them, he later said, 'much as an earnest Catholic must feel about wicked Popes'. From 1901 to 1906 he laboured hard on trying to find a way round them. Many times he thought he had found a solution, only to find that the contradiction, lke a cancerous growth, reappeared when he thought he had cut it out. He was helped in this work by his old tutor in mathematics, Alfred North Whitehead, with whom he had agreed to produce a joint work that would fulfil the promise of *The Principles of Mathematics* by actually carrying out, theorem by theorem, the reduction of mathematics to logic. Eventually, this collaboration produced the massive – and almost completely unreadable – classic three-volumed work *Principia Mathematica*, which was published from 1909 to 1913.

The system of logic contained in *Principia Mathematica* is a far cry indeed from the one envisaged by Russell in *The Principles of Mathematics*. In place of the beautifully clear and simple theory of classes that Russell had considered to be the essence of mathematics, Russell and Whitehead created a system of quite monstrous complexity. Many of the complications introduced to the theory were forced upon them by the need to avoid paradoxes, but others were motivated by Russell's rapidly changing philosophical views. Broadly speaking, the change in Russell's philosophical outlook between *Principles* and *Principia* might be characterized as a shift from ontology to semantics, from questions about what does and does not exist to questions about what it does and does not make sense to say. In the process, he was forced to embark on what he later described as 'the retreat from Pythagoras'.

The retreat was gradual and, as we shall see, traces of Platonism (or Pythagoreanism) survive even in *Principia*. How reluctant he was to give up the Pythagorean mysticism that had inspired his work on mathematics is shown clearly in an article he wrote a year after his discovery of the paradox called 'The Study of Mathematics', in which he speaks of the objective truths of mathematics still in the exalted tones of a devout believer:

Mathematics, perhaps more even than the study of Greece and Rome, has suffered from oblivion of its due place in civilization. Although tradition has decreed that the great bulk of educated men shall know at least the elements of the subject, the reasons for which the tradition arose are forgotten, buried beneath a great rubbish heap of pedantries and trivialities. To those who inquire as to the purpose of mathematics, the usual answer will be that it facilitates the making of machines, the travelling from place to place, and the victory over foreign nations, whether in war or commerce ... yet it is none of these that entitles mathematics to a place in every liberal education. Plato, we know, regarded the contemplation of mathematical truths as worthy of the Deity; and Plato realized, more perhaps than any other single man, what those elements are in human life which merit a place in heaven.

... Mathematics, rightly viewed, possesses not only truth, but supreme beauty – a beauty cold and austere, like that of sculpture, without appeal to any part of our weaker nature, without the gorgeous trappings of painting or music, yet sublimely pure, and capable of stern perfection such as only the greatest art can show. The true spirit of delight, the exaltation, the sense of being more than man, which is the touchstone of the highest excellence, is to be found in mathematics as surely as poetry ... Real life is, to most men, a long second-best, a perpetual compromise between the ideal and the possible; but the world of pure reason knows no compromise, no practical limitations, no barrier to the creative activity embodying in splendid edifices the passionate aspiration after the perfect from which all great work springs.

... Of the austerer virtues the love of truth is the chief, and in mathematics, more than elsewhere, the love of truth may find encouragement for waning faith.

(*ML*, 62–74)

Russell's determination to hold onto this exalted view faced two considerable problems: 1, he had to show that the 'splendid edifices' of mathematics were soundly built, even after the foundations he had intended to give them had developed major cracks; and 2, he had to answer the question of what, if classes and numbers were 'fictions', Plato's Deity was thinking about when He contemplated the 'truths of mathematics'.

As Russell wrestled with these questions, he embarked on

a programme of savagely pruning his ontology, concluding time and time again that what he had thought were 'things' were in fact just words or symbols, signifying nothing. First classes (and therefore numbers), then definite descriptions, and then propositions themselves were declared by him to be 'incomplete symbols'. The assumption guiding this pruning was that, if a symbol were 'complete' – i.e., meaningful – there would be an object corresponding to it. The cornerstone of his thinking about classes, it will be remembered, was that to every meaningful propositional function there corresponded a class. Russell now subjected this assumption to rigorous examination, putting stricter and stricter limits on what counted as meaningful in the light of his increasingly *un*-Pythagorean conception of what kinds of things exist. The first to go were classes. There are no such things and therefore the question as to whether a class does or does not belong to itself does not arise: the question is nonsense. But, if classes do not exist, upon what do the foundations of mathematics now stand? Russell's provisional answer was: propositional functions. Just as every statement about numbers can be analysed as being about classes, every statement about classes can be analysed as being about propositional functions. As Russell put it in *Lectures on Logical Atomism*:

> I have been talking, for brevity's sake, as if there really were all these different sorts of things [numbers, classes, classes of classes, etc.]. Of course, that is nonsense. There are particulars, but when one comes on to classes, and classes of classes, and classes of classes of classes,

one is talking of logical fictions ... what are the sort of things you would like to say about classes? They are just the same as the sort of things you want to say about propositional functions. You want to say of a propositional function that is is sometimes true. That is the same thing as saying of a class that it has members. You want to say that it is true for exactly 100 values of the variables. That is the same as saying of a class that it has a hundred members. All the things you want to say about classes are the same as the things you want to say about propositional functions excepting for accidental and irrelevant linguistic forms ... In that way you find that all the formal properties that you desire of classes, all their formal uses in mathematics, can be obtained without supposing for a moment that there are such things as classes, without supposing, that is to say, that a proposition in which symbolically a class occurs, does in fact contain a constituent corresponding to that symbol, and when rightly analysed that symbol will disappear.

(*LA*, 136–8)

In the light of such considerations, Russell made central to his philosophy a kind of analysis that sought to reveal the *real* logical form that lies hidden behind 'accidental and irrelevant linguistic forms'. 'The problem that there is arises from our inveterate habit of trying to name what cannot be named', he said. 'If we had a proper logical language, we should not be tempted to do that.' His and Whitehead's task, then, was to construct such a 'proper logical language', a language in which there would be no symbols for numbers or classes, but only for particulars and propositional functions. As a matter of convenience, symbols for numbers and classes would be introduced, but a systematic and rigorous technique would be provided for translating them back into a more 'logically proper' form, and cautions would be issued that the things these symbols *appear* to name do not actually exist.

The most celebrated example of this kind of analysis in Russell's work is his Theory of Descriptions, first published in an article called 'On Denoting' in 1905. Russell's purpose in developing this theory was closely tied to his efforts to repair the damage done to his philosophy of mathematics by the Paradox – and in particular to his efforts to remove classes from his ontology – but this aspect of the theory tends now to be forgotten. 'Denoting' is the word that Russell gave in *The Principles of Mathematics* to the logical relation between a concept and an object, class, or number (these, of course, not being distinct categories in *Principles*, for at that stage in Russell's thought a number was a class and a class was an object). Thus, the concept 'the first woman Prime Minister of Great Britain' denotes Margaret Thatcher; 'the next prime after 7' denotes the number 11; 'all even numbers' denotes the infinite class of even numbers, etc. Denotation is rather different from the notion of *reference* with which it is often confused; reference is a linguistic relation between a word or string of words and an object, for example between a name and a person. On Russell's theory, names do not denote; what denotes is a *concept* and in language denotation is achieved by means, not of a name, but of a *description*. More especially, in *Principles of Mathematics*, denotation is achieved by a description that begins with one of the following six words: *all*, *every*, *any*, *a*, *some* and *the*.

The importance of denotation for Russell is that denoting phrases are central to mathematics (*the* square root of 2', '*all* even numbers are the sum of 2 primes', etc.) and also that denotation and propositional functions go hand in hand with each other. As he put it in *Lectures on Logical Atomism*: 'Whenever you get such words as "a", "some", "all", "every", it is always a mark of the presence of a propositional function.' So, for example, for Russell the statement 'All dogs are dirty' would be understood as asserting that the propositional function, 'if x is a dog, x is dirty' is always true, 'I met a man' as asserting that the propositional function 'I met x and x is human' is not always false, and so on. Just as, at the time of writing *Principles*, Russell held that every meaningful propositional function defined a class (even if the class was empty), so he believed that every meaningful denoting phrase denoted *something*, even some 'thing' that did not exist. Now, taking a sterner line on existence, Russell held that things that did not exist were nothing at all, and that denoting phrases that *appeared* to denote non-existent things were, in fact, meaningless.

In 'On Denoting' Russell undertook to analyse statements containing denoting phrases in such a way as to remove altogether the appearance of denoting things that did not exist. The theory he advanced is that *all* denoting phrases are, in themselves, meaningless. They are 'incomplete symbols' that only acquire a meaning in the context of a proposition. Take, for example, definite descriptions (phrases beginning with the word 'the'): 'the present King of France', 'the next prime after 7', etc. These phrases, Russell now held, do not mean anything. However, statements containing them *do* mean something, but *what* they mean can only properly be understood when they are translated in such a way that the definite description does not occur. Take, for example, the statement, 'The present King of France is bald.' This appears to assume, falsely, that there *is*, at present, a King of France and, moreover, it appears to denote this non-existent entity and to predicate baldness of it. Russell's proposed translation transforms this assumption into an explicit statement. According to his Theory of Descriptions, 'The Present King of France is bald' is *really* a conjunction of three assertions:

1. The propositional, 'x is at present King of France' is not always false.
2. If the propositional function 'y is at present King of France' is true for any y, then y is identical to x [i.e., there is only *one* present King of France]
3. x is bald.

The first assertion amounts to an explicit statement that the present King of France exists and as this is false, the entire conjunction is false. So, by means of this rather convoluted analysis, 'The present King of France is bald' is shown to be a meaningful, but false, proposition.

In Russell's 'logically proper language', then, denoting phrases do not occur. There is, contrary to what he had said in *Principles*, no such thing as denotation (in a way, this follows immediately from the denial of the existence of classes, for in most cases the 'denoted object' was a class). Instead of denotation, what we have are statements to the effect that a given propositional function ('x is F') is always true, always false, or sometimes true ('not always false'). This last becomes, in effect, a statement of existence. To say that angels exist, for example, is to say that the propositional function 'x is an angel' is sometimes true.

Russell's determination to do away with classes and rest his entire theory on propositional functions is, in some ways, rather odd. For, as he realized at a fairly early stage, the paradox of classes that do or do not belong to themselves has its analogue in the realm of propositional functions, where the problem is caused by propositions which are, or are not, *true* of themselves. He seemed to think that propositional functions were somehow more manageable than classes. In any case, he was by now convinced on quite general philosophical grounds – independently, that is, of the formal problem of constructing a consistent theory of logic and mathematics – that classes do not exist. A further step in his ontological pruning was taken soon after writing 'On Denoting', when he became convinced on similar grounds that there were no such 'things' as propositions.

Until 1907, Russell conceived of propositions as being, in some sense, abstract objects. Propositions, for him, were not sentences; they were not, that is, units of language, they were the objects of thoughts. Thus, if I think that 2 plus 2 is 4, and so do you, then '2 + 2 = 4' is the proposition to which both our thoughts refer. This proposition has some kind of objective status; it has its being, that is, not in my mind or yours, but in, so to speak, the realm of truth. For a short while, after he had eliminated numbers and classes, Russell made this notion the basis of a vestigial Platonism about mathematics, which he described in a letter to his friend Margaret Llewelyn Davies on 26 March 1906:

> I did not mean [in his article, 'The Study of Mathematics'] that the objects of mathematics or other abstract thoughts *exist* outside us, still less that there is any universal or divine mind whose ideas we are reproducing when we think. What I meant to say was that the object of any abstract thought is not a thought, either of the thinker or of any one else, and does not *exist* at all, though it *is* something. Thus in mathematics a new theorem is a *discovery* in the sense that the discoverer for the first time apprehends the fact discovered, which fact has a timeless *being*, not *existence*.

This distinction between 'being' and 'existence', however, sat uncomfortably with Russell's new-found ontological austerity, and the same force that impelled him to abandon the non-existent 'things' denoted by definite descriptions impelled him also to get rid of propositions. If something does not exist, then it cannot *be* anything. This was brought home to Russell by reflecting upon *false* propositions. The idea that '2 + 2 = 4' *is* something, that it has 'a timeless being', has some plausibility, especially to someone with vestiges of a Pythagorean belief in the timeless world of arithmetical truth. But, what if you and I both thought that 2 plus 2 was 5? Would the object of that thought too have a timeless being? With a ruthlessness typical of the way he treated his earlier opinions, Russell came to ridicule the view:

> Time was when I thought there were propositions, but it does not seem to me very plausible to say that in addition to facts there are also these curious shadowy things going about such as 'That today is Wednesday' when it is in fact Tuesday. I cannot believe they go about in the real world. It is more than one can manage to believe, and I do think no person with a vivid sense of reality can imagine it. (*LA*, 87)

Propositions, then, do not exist and therefore sentences expressing propositions have to be regarded, like definite descriptions, as 'incomplete symbols', only now the context that is required to make them significant is a person's mind. Propositions do not mean anything until they are *judged* true or false by someone. The judgement is true if it corresponds with the facts and false otherwise. Thus, facts exist 'in the world' and thoughts exist 'in the head', but propositions, 'these curious shadowy things' that were alleged to be somewhere between the two, have no existence whatever. In the Introduction to *Principia Mathematica*, Russell expresses the point like this:

> What we call a 'proposition' (in the sense in which this is distinguished from the phrase expressing it) is not a single entity at all. That is to say, the phrase which expresses a proposition is what we call an 'incomplete'

symbol; it does not have meaning in itself, but requires some supplementation in order to acquire a complete meaning ... Thus 'the proposition "Socrates is human"' uses 'Socrates is human' in a way which requires a supplement of some kind before it acquires a complete meaning; but when I judge 'Socrates is human' the meaning is completed by the act of judging, and we no longer have an incomplete symbol. The fact that propositions are 'incomplete symbols' is important philosophically, and is relevant at certain points in symbolic logic. (*PM*, 44)

What, then *is* a judgement? Clearly not a relation between a mind and a proposition, for if propositions do not exist, they cannot stand in any kind of relation with anything. In the face of this, Russell developed what he called the 'multiple relation theory of judgement', according to which a judgement is a series of relations between a mind and the *constituents* of a proposition. Thus, the judgement 'Socrates is mortal' is a series of relations between three things: the individual, Socrates, the predicate 'mortality', and the mind that brings them together to judge that Socrates is mortal.

Having eliminated numbers, classes, denoting phrases and propositions, Russell was left with a horribly complicated 'logically proper language', in which even the simplest mathematical formula would be expressed in an almost incomprehensibly convoluted manner. But worse was to come, for he had still not solved the paradox, which, he now came to think, had its roots in the possibility of *self-reference*. Cantor's Paradox of the largest cardinal and hi own paradox of the class of classes which do not contain themselves were, he believed, variants of the old paradox of the Cretan who says 'All Cretans are liars': if he is telling the truth, then he is lying and if he is lying, then he is telling the truth. The problem, of course, is generated by the fact that his sentence includes itself. In a logically perfect language, therefore, it should be impossible for a judgement to include itself. This is the basic idea behind the Theory of Types that Russell built into the logical system of *Principia Mathematica*.

Expressed, for a moment, in terms of logical fictions, the Theory of Types says that there is a hierarchy of objects: first particulars, then classes, then classes of classes, and so on. A class can only be constructed of the objects on one particular level of the hierarchy, namely, the level immediately below itself, so a class cannot include itself. It follows immediately, of course, that there is no such thing as the class of all classes and that therefore neither Cantor's paradox, nor Russell's, applies to the system. But, of course, classes do not exist, so the Theory of Types has to be expressed instead in terms of propositional functions, and now it says that a propositional function is *meaningless* if it takes itself as a value of its variable (i.e., a proposition cannot meaningfully refer to itself). The hierarchy now becomes one of propositions and propositional functions: at the bottom level are elementary propositions containing no variables; at the next level are propositional functions whose variables range only over particulars; then propositional functions that can take other, lower-level propositional functions as their values, etc. At this point, the Theory of Types becomes what Russell always claimed it was, namely a 'theory of symbolism'. Of course, to be philosophically scrupulous, propositions do not exist either, so ultimately the Theory of Types has to be regarded as establishing different levels of judgements.

From a formal point of view, the system of logic outlined in *Principia Mathematica* is one of quite dizzying complexity. It has been said that it is probably the most complicated structure ever invented by a single human mind (for, though Whitehead collaborated with Russell on the mathematical parts of the enterprise, the Theory of Types was Russell's own). Statements about number are reduced to statements about classes, which are, in turn, reduced to the theory of propositional functions, which is, ultimately grounded in the Theory of Types. So many definitions and preliminary theorems are needed before arithmetic can get started that, for example, the proposition '1 plus 1 is 2' is arrived at only halfway through Volume II.

But philosophically, the picture is, if anything, still more murky. When Russell believed in classes, it was fairly clear what the point was of reducing mathematics to logic: it was to show that the truths of mathematics were a part of the larger realm of objective logical truth. This still, of course, is the purpose of *Principia Mathematica*, but it is now much less clear what the 'objects' are that inhabit the realm of logical truth. It is easy to say what they are not. They are not numbers, classes, or propositions. Can one say, perhaps, that they are *forms*? In an unfinished paper called 'What is Logic?' that he wrote soon after the completion of *Principia*, Russell struggled to make this idea plausible. '*

form is something', he wrote, and yet the paper shows him at a loss to explain what kind of 'thing' it is.

By 1913, Russell became persuaded by his brilliant young student, Ludwig Wittgenstein, that there were no such things as logical objects, and yet he still insisted that there *was* such a thing as logical knowledge. This, according to Russell's epistemology at the time, required there to be such a thing as *acquaintance* in logic, acquaintance being, in other contexts, a direct relation between ourselves and the objects of our knowledge. Again, Russell struggled with the obvious inconsistency. 'Logical objects cannot be regarded as "entities"', he wrote, and yet there *must* be 'something which seems fitly described as "acquaintance with logical objects".'

Between 1914 and 1917, Russell abandoned philosophy in favour of campaigning against the First World War, but in the summer of 1917 he returned once more to the question of what, if anything, the objects of logic are. In this, he was inspired to some extent by the encouragement of his friend, the mathematician Philip Jourdain, who urged him to write a series of articles under the title, 'What is Logic?' 'I want to know badly what logic is', Jourdain wrote. In *Introduction to Mathematical Logic*, written the following year, Russell took up the question and answered that logic was 'concerned with the real world just as truly as zoology, though with its more abstract and general featur- es'. What he meant is explained to some extent in *Lectures on Logical Atomism*, written the same year. Logic, he says there, is 'concerned with the forms of facts, with getting hold of the different sorts of facts, different *logical* sorts of facts, that there are in the world'. But are these forms 'objects' in any sense? Well, in any case, Russell seems to suggest that they can – with great difficulty – be made the objects of our thoughts, and that they are distinct from the symbols we use to represent them. Logic *does* have its own subject-matter, only it is a very rarefied and elusive one:

> [In philosophical logic] the subject-matter that you are supposed to be thinking of is so exceedingly difficult and elusive that any person who has ever tried to think about it knows that you do not think about it except perhaps once in six months for half a minute. The rest of the time you think about the symbols, because they are tangible, but the thing you are supposed to be thinking about is fearfully difficult and one does not often manage to think about it. The really good philosopher is the one who does once in six months think about it for a minute. Bad philosophers never do.   (*LA*, 44)

Within a year, having in the meantime read Wittgenstein's *Tractatus Logico-Philosophicus*, Russell abandoned this view. The reason it is so difficult to distinguish the symbols of logic from what they represent, he now came to think, is because there is no difference. 'Logic and the so-called "Laws of Thought"', he now roundly declared 'are concerned with symbols; they give different ways of saying the same thing ... only an understanding of language is necessary in order to know a proposition of logic.' A logical principle, he wrote, asserts nothing but 'that this symbol and that have the same meaning', adding: 'I have adopted this view from Mr Wittgenstein.'

The 'retreat from Pythagoras' was now complete: logical forms, like numbers, classes and propositions, were consigned to the wastepaper basket of metaphysical illusions. Russell still believed that mathematics was reducible to logic, but what this showed, he now believed, is that it is concerned only with 'different ways of saying the same thing':

> Mathematics has ceased to seem to me non-human in its subject-matter. I have come to believe, though very reluctantly, that it consists of tautologies. I fear that, to a mind of sufficient intellectual power, the whole of mathematics would appear trivial, as trivial as the statement that a four-footed animal is an animal ... I cannot any longer find any mystical satisfaction in the contemplation of mathematical truth ... I have no longer the feeling that intellect is superior to sense, and that only Plato's world of ideas gives access to the 'real' world.   (MPD, 211–12)

Indeed, it now became important to Russell *not* to believe in the world of ideas, a belief he now began to ridicule as a morbid dislike of the real world.

Ironically, shortly after Russell abandoned the last traces of his Pythagoreanism on the grounds that mathematics had been shown to be nothing more than logic and, therefore, linguistic, a proof was published that threw serious doubt upon the supposed reduction of mathematics to logic. This was the famous Gödel Incompleteness Proof, first published in January 1931 in a paper called 'On Formally Undecidable Propositions of *Principia Mathematica* and Related Systems'. In it, Gödel provided a strict formal proof that what Russell and Whitehead had tried to achieve in *Principia Mathematica* could never be fully realized: there cannot, in principle, be a single system of logic in which the whole of mathematics can be derived. Gödel himself was a Platonist, and he and others regarded his proof as providing some support for the Platonist view.

Russell was surprisingly slow to react to Gödel's proof. When, in 1937, he produced a new edition of *The Principles of Mathematics*, he wrote a new Introduction that discussed some of the work done in the area since 1903, but he conspicuously failed to mention Gödel. In 1942, however, Gödel was commissioned to write an article for the volume on Russell in Paul Schilpp's series *The Library of Living Philosophers*, and took the opportunity to combat what he considered to be the baleful influence of Wittgenstein on Russell's philosophy of mathematics. His article, 'Russell's Mathematical Logic', criticizes Russell for his abandonment of classes in *Principia Mathematica* and argues for the kind of Platonic conception of mathematics with which Russell had begun. Classes, says Gödel, may indeed be regarded as real objects: 'It seems to me that the assumption of such objects is quite as legitimate as the assumption of physical bodies and there is quite as much reason to believe in their existence.'

Russell, however, was not to be drawn into the debate that Gödel had hoped to provoke. He replied to all the essays published in the Schilpp volume *except* Gödel's, to which he responded only with the lame remark: 'His [Gödel's] great ability, as shown in his previous work, makes me think it highly probable that many of his criticisms of me are justified.' Soon afterwards, however, he met Gödel himself at Princeton, and seemed surprised to find that Gödel 'turned out to be an unadulterated Platonist, and apparently believed that an eternal "not" was laid up in heaven where virtuous logicians might hope to meet it hereafter'. To this, Gödel responded that his own Platonism was no more 'unadulterated' than Russell's had been when he talked, for example, of logic being concerned with the real world just as truly as zoology: 'At that time evidently Russell had met the "not" even in this world, but later on under the influence of Wittgenstein he chose to ignore it.'

Russell never did respond in detail to Gödel's arguments for Platonism. Perhaps they came too late for him; he was nearly sixty when the Incompleteness Theorem was published and over seventy when asked to reply to Gödel's essay for Schilpp. In any case, his mind was made up: the Platonic world of objective mathematical truth was an illusion. In one of his very last philosophical essays, written in 1951 and called 'Is Mathematics Purely Linguistic?', he, as it were, laid a wreath on the tomb of his early hopes for mathematics:

> Pythagoras, and Plato after him, had a theory of mathematics as charming as it was simple ... Pythagoras thought that mathematics is the study of numbers, and that each number is a separate eternal entity dwelling in a super-sensible heaven. When I was young I believed something like this ... But study gradually dispelled this

belief ... it turns out that numbers are nothing but a verbal convenience, and disappear when the propositions that seem to contain them are fully written out. To look for numbers in heaven is therefore as futile as to look for (say) 'etc'.

... All the propositions of mathematics and logic are assertions as to the correct use of a small number of words.

This conclusion, if valid, may be regarded as an epitaph on Pythagoras. (*EA*, 300–6)

At about the same time, Russell wrote a short story which dramatized the intellectual road he had travelled in his thinking about mathematics. It is called 'The Mathematician's Nightmare', and tells the story of 'Professor Squarepunt', who 'worn out by a long day's study of the old theories of Pythagoras' falls asleep in his chair, 'where a strange drama visited his sleeping thoughts':

The numbers, in this drama, were not the bloodless categories that he had previously supposed them: They were living breathing beings endowed with all the passions which he was accustomed to find in his fellow mathematicians. In his dream he stood at the centre of endless concentric circles. The first circle contained the numbers from 1 to 10; the second, those from 11 to 100; the third, those from 101 to 1,000; and so on, illimitably, over the infinite surface of a boundless plain. The odd numbers were male; the evens, female. Beside him in the centre stood Pi, the Master of Ceremonies. Pi's face was masked, and it was understood that none could behold it and live. But piercing eyes looked out from the mask, inexorable, cold, and enigmatic. Each number had its name clearly marked upon its uniform. Different kinds of numbers had different uniforms and different shapes: the squares were tiles, the cubes were dice, round numbers were balls, prime numbers were indivisible cylinders, perfect numbers had crowns.

… The numbers danced round Professor Squarepunt and Pi in a vast and intricate ballet … At a sign from Pi the ballet ceased, and the numbers one by one were introduced to Professor Squarepunt. Each number made a little speech explaining its peculiar merits.

… [After a while] the mathematician got bored and turned to Pi, saying: 'Don't you think the rest of the introductions could be taken for granted?' At this there was a general outcry.

… There was such a din that the mathematician covered his ears with his hands and turned an imploring gaze upon Pi. Pi waved his conductor's baton and proclaimed in a voice of thunder: 'Silence! Or you shall all become incommensurable'. All turned pale and submitted.

Throughout the ballet the Professor had noticed one number among the primes, 137, which seemed unruly and unwilling to accept its place in the series … At length 137 exclaimed: 'There's a damned sight too much bureaucracy here! What I want is liberty for the individual.' Pi's mask frowned. But the Professor interceded, saying, 'Do not be too hard on him … I should like to hear what 137 has to say.'

Somewhat reluctantly, Pi consented. Professor Square-punt said: 'Tell me, 137, what is the basis of your revolt?' ... At this, 137 burst into excited speech: 'It is their metaphysic that I cannot bear. They still pretend that they are eternal, though long ago their conduct showed that they think no such thing. We all found Plato's heaven dull and decided that it would be more fun to govern the sensible world. Since we descended from the Empyrean we have had emotions not unlike yours: each Odd loves its attendant Even; and the Evens feel kindly towards the Odds, in spite of finding them very odd. Our empire now is of this world, and when the world goes pop, we shall pop too.'

Professor Squarepunt found himself in agreement with 137. But all the others, including Pi, considered him a blasphemer, and turned upon both him and the Professor. The infinite host, extending in all directions farther than the eye could reach, hurled themselves upon the poor Professor in an angry buzz. For a moment he was terrified. Then he pulled himself together and, suddenly recollecting his waking wisdom, he called out in stentorian tones: 'Avaunt! You are only Symbolic Conveniences!'

With a banshee wail, the whole vast array dissolved in mist. And, as he woke, the Professor heard himself saying, 'So much for Plato!'   (*NEP*, 48–53)

The 'Pythagorean Dream', Russell came finally to think, had been nothing but a nightmare all along.